CONTENTS

To access audio visit:
www.halleonard.com/mylibrary

"Enter Code"
4943-7697-0471-5470

Audio Arrangements by Peter Deneff

ISBN 978-1-4950-2306-4

HAL•LEONARD®
CORPORATION
7777 W. BLUEMOUND RD. P.O. BOX 13819 MILWAUKEE, WI 53213

Visit Hal Leonard Online at
www.halleonard.com

ALL ABOUT THAT BASS

TROMBONE

Words and Music by KEVIN KADISH
and MEGHAN TRAINOR

ALL OF ME

TROMBONE

Words and Music by JOHN STEPHENS
and TOBY GAD

To Coda

D.S. al Coda

CODA

mp

mf

p

HAPPY

from DESPICABLE ME 2

Words and Music by
PHARRELL WILLIAMS

TROMBONE

RADIOACTIVE

TROMBONE

Words and Music by DANIEL REYNOLDS,
BENJAMIN McKEE, DANIEL SERMON,
ALEXANDER GRANT and JOSH MOSSER

ROAR

TROMBONE

Words and Music by KATY PERRY,
LUKASZ GOTTWALD, MAX MARTIN,
BONNIE McKEE and HENRY WALTER

To Coda ⊕

D.S. al Coda

CODA ⊕

2

mf

f

SAY SOMETHING

TROMBONE

Words and Music by IAN AXEL,
CHAD VACCARINO and MIKE CAMPBELL

SOMEONE LIKE YOU

TROMBONE

Words and Music by ADELE ADKINS
and DAN WILSON

SHAKE IT OFF

TROMBONE

Words and Music by TAYLOR SWIFT,
MAX MARTIN and SHELLBACK

D.S. al Coda

CODA

A SKY FULL OF STARS

TROMBONE

Words and Music by GUY BERRYMAN,
JON BUCKLAND, WILL CHAMPION,
CHRIS MARTIN and TIM BERGLING

Moderate Dance groove

To Coda

THINKING OUT LOUD

TROMBONE

Words and Music by ED SHEERAN
and AMY WADGE

UPTOWN FUNK

TROMBONE

Words and Music by MARK RONSON,
BRUNO MARS, PHILIP LAWRENCE,
JEFF BHASKER, DEVON GALLASPY
and NICHOLAUS WILLIAMS

STAY WITH ME

TROMBONE

Words and Music by SAM SMITH,
JAMES NAPIER and WILLIAM EDWARD PHILLIPS

Moderately